WHEELS

Cars, cogs, carousels and other things that spin

Words by Tracey Turner   **Art by Fatti Burke**

This book is for all the children:
Toby, Josh, Ollie, Sasha, Jasper, Maddy, Will.

WHEELS

Cars, cogs, carousels and other things that spin

Words by Tracey Turner   Art by Fatti Burke

KINGFISHER

A Raspberry Book
Editorial: Kath Jewitt
Art direction: Sidonie Beresford-Browne
Cover design: Sidonie Beresford-Browne
Internal design: Peter Clayman
Consultant: Jack Challoner

KINGFISHER

First published 2019 by Kingfisher
an imprint of Macmillan Children's Books
a division of Macmillan Publishers International Limited
The Smithson, 6 Briset Street, London EC1M 5NR
Associated companies throughout the world
www.panmacmillan.com

ISBN 978-0-7534-4490-0

9 8 7 6 5 4 3 2 1
1TR/0819/WKT/UG/128MA

A CIP catalogue record for this book is available from the British Library.

Printed in China

Contents

Landing would be a lot easier with wheels!

Introduction

Wheels are the work of genius, and they have completely changed the world. You might have found them useful on wheelchairs, bikes, buses, trains, cars and planes. They move things about for us in trucks and wheelbarrows. They make pottery and spin cloth. They fit together as gears to make all sorts of machines work, and they got the first clocks ticking.

As well as being useful, wheels are fun.
They whizz us around on roller coasters, carousels,
Ferris wheels, roller skates, skateboards and scooters.
And if you think you'd be bored without wheels,
just imagine how pet hamsters would feel.

Life would be dull without Wheeeels!

But wheels haven't always been around, and they were tricky to invent. There aren't any wheels in the natural world to give people the idea, so making a disk with a hole in the middle and a rod going through it – a wheel and axle – was an amazingly clever idea. In some parts of the world, wheels were never invented: in the Americas, people managed without wheels completely, apart from on toys in Ancient Mexico.

So let's give the inventor of the wheel an absolutely massive round of applause. Then climb aboard, buckle up your seatbelt and perhaps put on a safety helmet, just in case. It's time to discover the wonder of wheels.

Find out what the world's largest vehicle has in common with Big Ben.

Learn how to ride downhill on a penny-farthing.

Discover some of the most useful, fun and unusual wheels in the world!

Potters' Wheels

Potters' wheels were the very first wheels of all. Even before they moved carts, wheels were used to make pots.

By around 5000 years ago, potters' wheels could be turned by a second wheel, which was operated with the foot. The wheels spun much more quickly, so that potters could throw a lump of clay onto the wheel and use their fingers to shape the pot.

Pottery was made by coiling strips of clay and pressing them together, until potters realized that things would be a lot easier if the pot could be spun around. The first potters' wheels, invented around 6500 years ago, were moveable platforms that were turned by hand.

The faster wheels were a breakthrough, because now lots of pots could be made to the same design in a short space of time – as long as the potter was skilful enough.

Modern potters can use a wheel powered by an electric motor, but some prefer to use human power, just like potters thousands of years ago.

Clay Babies
In Ancient Egypt, Khnum was god of the source of the River Nile. People believed he made human children on a potter's wheel, out of clay taken from the river bed.

It looks a lot easier than it is!

Even huge great pots can be made on a wheel, though the biggest ones have to be made in sections. Pots like the one below were made in Athens, Ancient Greece, more than 2000 years ago. An artist used liquid clay to add the beautiful decorations.

The First Wheels

No one knows who invented the wheel, or even where it was invented. But thank goodness someone did.

Before there were wheels, moving heavy objects about was tiring and troublesome. Things were dragged along on sledges, which was hard work.

The earliest wheels ever found are around 5500 years old, and come from Central Europe and Western Asia.

Ooof! Phew!

Why didn't we think of this BEFORE we built that massive stone circle?

If the object was pushed and pulled along on top of logs laid next to one another, which rolled as the object moved forwards, it made the task a bit easier.

Ready to Roll

Putting logs underneath a heavy load keeps the load off the ground. When you push or pull the load, the logs roll. You can achieve the same result by attaching a wheel to an axle, and the axle to a cart that carries the load. But it's much better, because you don't have to keep moving the logs to the front once the object has passed over them.

The wheel and axle meant that people and their possessions could get about on carts pulled by horses or oxen. Now, people could travel and trade much more easily.

The first wheels were made of solid wood. Then someone had another bright idea – by adding spokes, wheels would be much lighter but still strong.

Chariots

⊛ ⊛ ⊛

Ancient chariots raced along on two spoked wheels, pulled by two or more horses. They were light and superfast, and originally made for war.

Chariot wheels need flat ground, so soldiers mounted on horses eventually became more common in battle. Chariots were used for fun instead – chariot racing was one of the events in the Olympic Games of Ancient Greece.

Out of my way!

The biggest chariot battle ever was the Battle of Kadesh, fought between the Egyptians and the Hittites in 1274 BCE. Between five and six thousand chariots took part.

The Ancient Romans absolutely loved chariot racing. The Circus Maximus in Ancient Rome was a huge chariot-racing track, or hippodrome, that could seat 150,000 spectators.

The chariots, driven by professional charioteers, hurtled around the corners and jostled for position. Accidents were common, and charioteers and horses were often seriously injured or killed.

In Ancient Rome, charioteers were divided into teams, and the teams could buy and sell them – just like football teams buy and sell players today. Spectators cheered on their teams with the same enthusiasm as today's football fans, and rivalry could be fierce.

Charioteers were usually slaves. Winning charioteers could become famous.

Horses could become famous too!

Circus seats were free in the Roman Empire, although wealthy people could pay for seats with shade and a good view. The Emperor had his own entrance to the Circus Maximus, directly connected to his palace.

Waterwheels

Around 2300 years ago, waterwheels were the first machines to use something other than human or animal power. They harnessed the power of flowing water to do all sorts of useful jobs.

There are different types of waterwheel. This one is driven by water that flows down onto the wheel from the pipe above it.

The wheel is made of wood or metal

Axle, which can be connected to other machinery with gears

Paddles or buckets arranged evenly around the outside of the wheel

Waterwheels are so useful because the energy in the turning wheel can be used to power other machinery, usually by a series of gears. Waterwheels can be used for...

- Lifting water, perhaps from a river to a field, to water crops

- Turning a big stone mill wheel, which grinds grain to make flour

- Driving bellows for forges and furnaces

- Mushing wood into pulp to make paper

- Driving pumps to keep mines dry (the Ancient Romans used waterwheels in mines, including copper mines in Spain and a gold mine in Wales)

Some waterwheels are still turning today. The Laxley Wheel in the Isle of Man, UK, is the biggest one in the world that is still used – it measures more than 22 metres across!

The modern equivalent of a waterwheel is the water turbine, which is used to generate electricity.

Thanks to wheels, we can all eat the bread made from this flour!

Cogs and Gears

Gears are wheels with teeth, called cogs, around the outside. The cogs of one gear fit together with cogs of another gear, and together they can make all sorts of useful machines.

If you turn this big gear, the smaller gear turns too, and in the opposite direction. So if the bigger gear turns clockwise, the smaller one will turn anticlockwise. The smaller gear will turn more quickly than the bigger gear.

How fast the small gear goes depends on the number of cogs! Clever. eh?

Gears can either increase speed or force, but not both.

A large gear driving a small gear increases speed.

A small gear driving a big gear increases force.

Gears can be put together in different combinations, and we use them every day. Bikes use gears attached to chains to increase the speed or force provided by the person pedalling. Cars use gears to increase the speed or force provided by the engine. Gears are used in all sorts of ways – in machines in factories, as well as in things that move.

Clockwork uses gears. Someone winds the key to provide the energy, then the energy is stored in a spring. Gears control how the energy is released – to move the hands on a clock, or to make a clockwork toy move.

Load-lifting Wheels
Wheels are also used in pulleys – a rope wound around a wheel with a grooved edge. Pulleys help to lift heavy loads.

Spinning Wheels

Wheels not only got people moving – they helped to keep people warm by spinning thread that could be woven into cloth.

Before there were big clothing factories, a spinner had to spin thread before a weaver could turn it into cloth. Then a tailor made the cloth into a cosy warm coat for when the weather got chilly.

At first, spinners used a stick with a hook on one end and a weight on the other. They attached the fleece to the hook and spun the stick. This pulled out the woolly fibres and twisted them together to make wool.

It's called a spindle. It works, but it takes quite a long time.

The wool is made from my fleece. Happy to help!

Spinning wheels were invented around 1500 years ago. They were much faster than spinning by hand. There are different types but they all work in a similar way: the spinner operates a treadle (foot pedal) to turn the wheel, which pulls the sheep's fleece from the spinner's hand and makes it into wool.

All sorts of thread can be made with a spinning wheel, including cotton and linen, which are made from cotton and flax plants.

It takes a while to learn, but now I'm superfast!

Later, steam-powered spinning machines were invented. These worked hundreds of times faster than individual spinning wheels, so huge amounts of thread could be produced very quickly.

Ancient Spinners

There was spinning in Greek mythology. The three Fates were goddesses who controlled human lives – one spun the thread of life, one measured it out and one cut it.

19

Colour Wheels

There's one type of wheel that can help you decorate your bedroom, paint a picture or decide what to wear.

Artists and designers use colour wheels to help choose which colours to use in their work. Most colour wheels have twelve sections, with a different colour in each one. There are three primary colours – normally red, yellow and blue – which can't be made from any other colour. Secondary and tertiary colours are made by mixing other colours together.

The colour wheel can be divided into 'warm' (top) and 'cool' (bottom) colours.

3
PRIMARY
COLOURS

3
PRIMARY
COLOURS
+3
SECONDARY
COLOURS

3 PRIMARY COLOURS

+ 3 SECONDARY COLOURS

+ 6 TERTIARY COLOURS

If you pick two colours on the wheel that are next to each other, mix them together and paint where the two colours meet, you'll get an in-between colour. You can make as many as you like – if you have a big enough wheel!

Colours opposite one another on the wheel make the biggest contrast – useful when you want to make words or pictures stand out. Other good colour combinations are any three evenly spaced colours, or two colours next to one another on the wheel with the two colours opposite them.

I'm using a colour from the opposite side of the wheel to make Monty's yellow fur stand out.

Woof!

All colours have tints, shades and tones: a tint is a colour mixed with white, a shade is a colour mixed with black, and a tone is a colour mixed with grey.

Ships' Wheels

⚓ ⚓ ⚓

Sometimes, things that float need wheels. These wheels are used to steer huge ships on the high seas.

Turning the wheel moves the ship's rudder, which is like a giant oar at the back of the ship underneath the water.

Just like cart wheels, a ship's wheel has an axle that goes through the centre, which controls the rudder. Handles around the outside of the wheel make it easy to control.

If I turn the wheel to the starboard, the ship moves to the right. Look out!

On a ship, 'starboard' means right and 'port' means left!

The ship travels in the direction that the wheel is turned. But the wheel turns the rudder in the opposite direction, because pushing the rudder to the right makes the ship move to the left, and pushing it to the left makes the ship move right.

Some ships have a double wheel – two wheels connected to each other. This allows two people to steer the ship in a storm, when one person alone might not be strong enough.

The ships' wheel was invented around the beginning of the 1700s. Before then, ships steered using a tiller – a wooden rod that moves the rudder.

squawk!

Cars Without Wheels

The first cars used tillers, until everybody realized that steering wheels made cars easier to control. The idea probably came from the ships' wheel.

Trains

Wheels that run on tracks are a great way to transport people and things. Trains pulled by locomotives have been chugging along for more than 200 years.

Rocket was an early steam-powered locomotive. It pulled trains on the world's first intercity railway, between Liverpool and Manchester in England. The steam engine was connected to the big front wheels, the smaller wheels at the back kept Rocket on the tracks.

LNER

Most of today's trains are powered by electricity or diesel, and some can go extremely fast. Japan's 'bullet trains', which appeared in the 1960s, were the very first high-speed trains. Today, high-speed trains run in lots of countries.

Freight trains are made to transport goods. They can be over 7 kilometres long and might need more than one locomotive to pull them.

In the USA, steam locomotives mostly used wood rather than coal as fuel. The sparks that flew out of the chimneys sometimes set fire to the countryside!

In the 1930s, the streamlined Mallard set the world speed record for a steam locomotive – 203 kilometres per hour.

The world train speed record is held by a French TGV train. It reached 575 kilometres per hour.

It wasn't long before trains went underground. The first underground railway opened in 1863 in London, and now there are around 180 in cities across the world.

Carousels

Without wheels we wouldn't have beautiful, whirling merry-go-rounds, and other spinning fairground rides.

Long before there were carousels, knights used to practise their skills by playing a game on wooden horses suspended from a pole, turned by a real horse or people. From the 1700s, carousels were built just for fun, but still needed animal or human power.

Carousels became really popular after steam-powered rides were invented. People whooshed around on beautifully carved, painted wooden horses at fairgrounds all over the world.

TICKETS

The base of a carousel is a big wheel turned on its side – the spinning axle in the middle turns the wheel using a system of pulleys and gears.

More gears make the horses go up and down as the carousel spins.

You can find all kinds of carousel animals, including tigers, giraffes and pigs. There's an insect-only carousel at the Bronx Zoo in New York, USA, where you can ride on a praying mantis or a dung beetle.

Lots of fairground rides are based on the same idea as carousels. In swing rides, passengers sit in chairs attached to chains, which swing out in a circle at up to 69 kilometres per hour high above the ground, as the ride spins. Playground roundabouts are simple, human-powered carousels.

A **loud** pipe organ plays automatically as the carousel turns.

Pardon?

As well as the gorgeous horses, paintings, mirrors and music help to make the carousel experience magical.

It's tricky to get on, difficult to get off and hard to ride without falling off.

Whoooaaaa!!

The Penny-Farthing

Penny-farthings were the first machines to be called bicycles. They're one of the world's oddest uses of wheels.

Penny-farthings could reach speeds of up to 40 kilometres per hour. They were fast because the big front wheel covered a lot of ground at each turn of the pedals.

The front wheel could measure nearly two metres across.

These strange-looking bikes whizzed along very fast indeed. There were a lot of nasty accidents – penny-farthings were hard to control. riders had a long way to fall and there were no brakes. Even so. these bicycles were popular for about 20 years in the 1870s and 1880s.

The penny-farthing was replaced by the 'safety bicycle' towards the end of the 1800s. and cycling became far less dangerous. This new invention had wheels of equal size and the pedals powered a chain attached to the back wheel.

Aaaargh!!

Going downhill on a penny-farthing was especially tricky. Riders put their legs over the handlebars and hoped to land on their feet if they fell off.

Pennies and Farthings
Penny-farthings got their name because of two coins that were in use at the time in Britain: a penny was a large coin, and a farthing was a much smaller one. The bikes were also called high-wheelers and ordinaries (even though they weren't).

1

The first powered cart was built by Nicolas-Joseph Cugnot in 1769. It was powered by steam, so it was enormous, heavy and slow.

During the twentieth century, cars began to sell in their millions after Henry Ford's factory in the USA made cheap, easy-to-run cars. His most famous was the Model T.

Steam Cars to Driverless Cars

Wheels were doing an excellent job of getting people about. But horses can only go so far and so fast, and people began to think of other ways to get wheels moving.

A Model T Ford could be made in about 90 minutes!

4

5

In the middle of the twentieth century, petrol was cheap and there was plenty of it, so cars became huge and extravagant.

Check out these wheels!

2 *I'll have you know that I also electrified the London Underground and Blackpool trams.*

Some early cars used electric motors, like this one made by Thomas Parker in 1884.

On the 200-kilometre trip I used my hatpin to clear a fuel line, and invented brake linings! **3**

The internal combustion engine, fuelled by petrol or diesel, became the most popular way to power cars. The first motor car with an engine was made by German engineer Karl Benz. His wife and business partner, Bertha Benz, made the world's first long-distance car journey in it.

6 Burning petrol and diesel pollutes the air and contributes to climate change, so companies have started to make electric cars again. The idea is that they're powered by electricity made using energy from the Sun, or in other sustainable ways.

All of these cars need a driver. But eventually, cars that can drive themselves will take over our roads. They'll be much safer than cars with human drivers.

Roller Coasters

If you like hurtling along upside-down at 240 kilometres per hour, you have yet another reason to be glad about wheels.

In Russia 500 years ago, brave riders whizzed down steep ice slides on sledges or wheeled carts. The idea reached France, where it isn't as cold, so waxed wooden slides were used instead of icy ones – the very first roller coasters.

In the United States, people in need of excitement paid to ride on a steep railway used for delivering coal. Later, America's first real roller coaster, the Switchback Railway, was built. The idea soon spread all over the world.

Stop! I left my stomach behind!
Aaaargh!!

Most roller coasters are made from steel.

Three Wheels

Modern roller coasters have three types of wheel. The wheels that go on top of the track make the roller coaster whizz along. The underneath and side wheels keep the roller coaster on the tracks.

Roller coasters continue to get bigger, faster and more stomach-churning . . . .

• Formula Rossa, United Arab Emirates, is the fastest roller coaster at 240 kilometres per hour.

• Kingda Ka, USA, is the tallest at 139 metres. Riders plummet 127 metres during the ride.

• Steel Dragon 2000, Japan, is the longest roller coaster at 2479 metres.

Today there are more than 4600 roller coasters in the world!
Wheeeeee!!

In some languages, roller coasters are called 'Russian mountains'.

Ferris Wheels

Ferris wheels are enormous, exciting, and absolute marvels of engineering.

Ferris wheels are named after George Ferris, who designed a huge, passenger-carrying wheel for the World's Fair in Chicago, USA, in 1893. The giant wheel was popular – more than a million passengers enjoyed the bird's-eye view from the top – and it earned US $736,000 (equal to about £15 million pounds today) in ticket sales. Sadly, George didn't profit from his invention, and died poor.

The original Ferris wheel was 80.4 metres high and had 36 wooden cars. Each car carried up to 60 passengers.

The axle weighed 42 tonnes and was the biggest single piece of steel ever made at the time.

You get a **great** view from up here!

The first Ferris wheel had fallen into disrepair by 1906. Dismantling it involved blowing it up with dynamite!

George Ferris's wheel wasn't a completely new idea. In Bulgaria in the 1600s, a wooden wheel with seats for passengers was turned by a very strong man, and there were similar fairground rides after that. None of them sound especially thrilling. But the Ferris wheel was enormous, made of steel, and the first to be properly fun.

There have been many more Ferris wheels since 1893. Today, the biggest one is twice the size of the original – the High Roller in Las Vegas, USA, stands at 167.6 metres tall.

Ferris wheels are extremely difficult and expensive to make. Much to everyone's disappointment, lots of Ferris wheels have been planned but abandoned part-way through.

Bicycles

Bicycles are an excellent way to travel because they keep you fit, don't pollute the atmosphere and convert human energy into movement more efficiently than anything else ever invented! There are lots of different kinds.

BMX, short for bicycle motocross, began as a pedal-power version of off-road motorcycling. BMX riders can perform amazing jumps and other stunts.

There are more than one billion bikes in the world, speeding people along on everyday journeys.

Whoooaaaa!!

Mountain bikes are good for off-road adventures. They have fatter tyres for rough ground, and low gears for steep hills.

Roller Skates and Skateboards

Roller skates and skateboards provide some of the best fun it is possible to have on wheels.

People have been whizzing about with wheels attached to their feet since the 1700s. The first roller skates were almost impossible to turn or stop, but better designs made roller skating safer and much more popular.

A roller-skating craze swept the United States in the 1860s and 1870s and spread to Europe. Since then, roller skating has never gone out of fashion.

Whizz!!

Zoom!!

People use skates as a fast and fun way to get about, but also compete in roller-skating sports, including speed skating, hockey and dancing. In the sport of roller derby, teams of skaters zoom around a rink in a fast and furious race, blocking the opposing team, slamming into one another and sending players flying.

In the middle of the twentieth century, skateboards were invented in California, USA. Because California is also famous for surfing, skateboarding used to be known as sidewalk surfing.

What you **really** need are wings!

If you need an excuse to jump on a skateboard, 21 June is Go Skateboarding Day.

You can use a skateboard to get you to school or to the shops, but skateboarders often learn tricks as well. An 'ollie' is one of the most basic tricks – lifting the board into the air while you're riding it. Once you've spent weeks mastering an ollie, you'll have the basis for all sorts of other moves.

There are thousands of skate parks around the world where you can demonstrate your tricks. The biggest is in Guangzhou, China – it covers an area the size of 65 tennis courts.

39

Racing Cars

Once wheels had engines attached to them, they were really good at going fast. Hardly any time at all after the first cars were made, people started racing them.

There are lots of different types of motor racing, with different types of cars and tracks. But they all have one thing in common: the cars zoom along at alarming speeds. Two of the fastest and most popular kinds of motor racing in the world are NASCAR and Formula 1, in which cars reach speeds of more than 340 kilometres per hour!

Racing drivers need excellent vision, coordination and reaction speeds...

In the United States, NASCAR stands for the National Association for Stock Car Racing. The cars look more like ordinary cars than racing cars, but they're lightning-fast. The most famous race is the Daytona 500, run over 800 kilometres in 200 laps around the Daytona International Speedway race course in Florida.

The most popular kind of motor racing. Formula 1 is an international competition. The 'formula' is a set of rules governing the size of the cars, engines, wheels and so on, that all the cars have to follow. One of the most famous races is the Monaco Grand Prix, where the cars screech around 78 laps of the streets of the city of Monte Carlo. There are other 'Formula' races, including Formula E for electric cars.

In the USA, IndyCar racing has millions of fans. The cars look similar to Formula 1 cars, with their wheels outside the body of the car, and go just as fast.

Really, Really Big Wheels

●●●●●

These are some of the biggest vehicles in the world – and of course they need really big wheels to move them about.

Monster trucks are famous for being huge. The biggest one of all is called Bigfoot. It weighs as much as three African elephants, it's taller than a double-decker bus and its tyres measure three metres across.

There's a longer monster truck – it's a monster limousine – that's nearly 10 metres long. But it's nowhere near as impressive!

BIGFOOT

This truck is not designed to go on roads – it's far too big! – but it does have an engine and can be driven. Anyone for a spin?

Even bigger than Bigfoot is the biggest pick-up truck in the world. This replica of a Dodge Power Wagon has a house inside it! It's about eight times as big as the original Dodge truck, weighs 50 tonnes and includes a living room, a kitchen, four bedrooms and a bathroom.

Road **hog!**

Normal-sized Dodge Power Wagon

But the biggest pick-up truck is just a baby compared to the largest land vehicle in the world. The Giant Bucket Wheel Excavator is a mining vehicle that works in a German coal mine. This immense vehicle also uses another wheel for digging – the bucket wheel at the front measures 21 metres across.

Giant Bucket Wheel Excavator

Height: 96 metres
(the same as Big Ben)

Width: 46 metres

Weight: 14,000 tonnes

Speed: very slow indeed

Wheels: 12 caterpillar-track wheels, each 3.8 metres wide

Wheel of Fortune

This imaginary wheel comes from ancient mythology and belongs to a goddess. It shows how easily human fortunes can change.

Who knows when I might feel like giving it a spin?
Whoops!

The goddess Fortuna spins her wheel at random – she's supposed not to know or care how her wheel affects people. It means good luck if the wheel turns and someone finds themselves at the top, but for the person opposite them at the bottom of the wheel, it means bad luck. In medieval times, the person at the top was usually represented by a king.

Someone at the height of wealth and happiness might be spun down to misery and poverty, or the other way around. **Whoa!**

Here we go again!

The zodiac is usually shown as a wheel, too: it's a collection of twelve star constellations through which the Sun passes over the course of a year. Just as medieval people believed that the Wheel of Fortune affected their lives, some people believe that the zodiac affects them – they think that the positions of the Sun, Moon and planets can change what happens in people's lives.

Today, the Wheel of Fortune is better known as a television game show! Contestants solve word puzzles, then a giant wheel is given a spin to reveal what prizes they win. The show began in the 1970s, and it's still watched in the USA today.

Timeline

Climb aboard our superfast time machine
for a quick spin through the history of wheels.

Around 4500 BCE

Potters' wheels were
the first wheels
ever invented.

Around 1300s

The first mechanical clocks,
using cogs and other wheels,
were invented.

Around 500 CE

Spinning wheels were invented,
so making textiles and clothes
became a lot quicker.

1666

Isaac Newton developed the
world's first colour wheel.

Around 1700

People used ships'
wheels to steer ship
for the first time.

1884

The first roller coaster, the
Switchback Railway, thrilled fair-
goers in the USA. It was designed
by LaMarcus Adna Thompson.

1872

The internal combustion
engine was invented by
George Brayton in the USA.

1893

The first Ferris wheel, named
after inventor George Ferris,
spun around in Chicago, USA.

1940s or '50s

The first skateboards were
invented in California, USA.

Around 3500 BCE

The earliest wheels on a vehicle date from 3500 BCE.

Around 2000 BCE

The first chariots, with spoked wheels, were pulled into battle by horses.

Around 250 BCE

...ears were used for predicting ...ositions of the Sun and Moon, in a machine made in Ancient Greece.

Around 300 BC

The first waterwheels were used – the first machines to use something other than human or animal power.

1861

The first steam-powered carousel was invented in England by Thomas Bradshaw.

1802

The first railway steam locomotive was invented by Richard Trevithick in England.

1869

The penny-farthing bicycle was invented by French engineer Eugène Meyer.

1863

The first underground railway, powered by steam, opened in London, UK.

1980s

The first driverless cars were developed.

2013

Four US states allowed driverless cars on public roads – the first in the world.

INDEX

Now that you know all about wheels, look out for a book about wings!